THE QUICK AND EASY PLANT-BASED DIET COOKBOOK

The Complete, Simple, and Quick Plant-Based

Cookbook to Save Time, and Live a Healthy Lifestyle

Tommy Adwell

Table of Contents

Introduction

If you're reading this book, then you're probably on a journey to get healthy because you know good health and nutrition go hand in hand.

Since what you eat fuels your body, you can imagine that eating junk will make you feel just that—like junk. I've followed the standard American diet for several years: my plate was loaded with high-fat and carbohydrate-rich foods. I know this doesn't sound like a horrible way to eat, but keep in mind that most Americans don't focus on eating healthy fats and complex carbs—we live on processed foods. The consequences of eating foods filled with trans fats, preservatives, and mountains of sugar are fatigue, reduced mental focus, mood swings, and weight gain, just to name but a few (The Nutrition Source, n.d.).

To top it off, there's the issue of opening yourself up to certain diseases—some life-threatening—when you neglect paying attention to what you eat (Center for Science in Public Interest, n.d.). To give you an idea, my husband suffered three strokes, my daughter is overweight at a young age, and I have hypertension and high cholesterol. The fact that I contributed to my family's health issues because I didn't do my research makes me feel somewhat like a failure as a wife and mother. So, I decided to find out more about what we were putting into our bodies.

That's why I decided to write this book: I want you armed with as much knowledge as possible about what I consider the healthiest alternative to the standard American diet. If you know about another option, you won't expect your family to eat takeout, microwave meals, or plates of food stacked with refined carbohydrates, heaps of protein, and little to no vegetables.

The guilt I felt caused me to spend hours researching what is considered good nutrition and looking for diets—or let's call them lifestyles—that fit the bill. As my research continued, one thing became clear: eating the American way is making thousands of people ill and shortening life spans every single day (Pritkin, n.d.). However, following a PLANT-BASED diet can reverse damage caused by unhealthy eating and add years to your life (Kerly, 2018).

After proper research, we decided as a family to change our lifestyle. No longer would it be based on convenience or cravings for foods packed with addictive sugar, but on following a more wholesome diet. Takeout meals, packaged and processed foods, and convenience meals were left off of the menu; instead, we focused on filling out plates with colorful fruits and vegetables and meat in the early days of our PLANT-BASED journey.

In this book, you'll read everything you need to know to transition from the standard American diet to a whole food plant-based diet. I'll share with you all the knowledge I have—based on research, as well as personal experience. I want to help you get healthy and live a happy and disease-free life for as long as possible. Furthermore, the recipes in this cookbook will make things easier for you as you learn to navigate PLANT-BASED cooking.

It's daunting when you start a new lifestyle—please use the knowledge and recipes in this book to help you succeed!

Recipes

Breakfast and Smoothies

1   Mango and Pineapple Smoothie

Preparation Time: 5 minutes

Cooking Time: 0 minutes

Serves 2

Ingredients:

- cups plant-based milk
- 1 frozen banana
- ½ cup frozen mango chunks
- ½ cup frozen pineapple chunks

- 1 teaspoon vanilla extract

Directions:

In a blender, combine the milk, banana, mango, pineapple, and vanilla. Blend on high for 1 to 2 minutes, or until the contents reach a smooth and creamy consistency, and serve.

Nutrition: Calories: 176 ; Fat: 4g; Carbs: 36g; Protein: 2g; Fiber: 4g

2 **Peanut Butter Banana Smoothie**

Preparation Time: 5 minutes

Cooking Time: 0 minutes

Servings: 2

Ingredients:

- frozen bananas, halved
- 1 cup plant-based milk
- 2 tablespoons defatted peanut powder
- 1 teaspoon vanilla extract
- ½ tablespoon chia seeds

Directions:

In a blender or food processor, combine the bananas, milk, peanut powder, and vanilla. Blend on high for 1 to 2 minutes.

Add the chia seeds, and pulse 2 to 4 times, or until the chia seeds have dispersed evenly without being blended up, and serve.

Nutrition: Calories: 271; Fat: 5g; Carbs: 47g; Protein: 11g; Fiber: 8g

3 <u>Apple and Walnut Bowl</u>

<u>*Preparation Time:*</u> 15 minutes

<u>*Cooking Time*</u>: 0 minutes

<u>*Servings*</u>: 4

<u>*Ingredients:*</u>

- 1 green apple, halved, seeded, and cored
- Honeycrisp apples, halved, seeded, and cored
- 1 teaspoon freshly squeezed lemon juice
- pitted Medjool dates
- ½ teaspoon ground cinnamon
- Pinch ground nutmeg

- 2 tablespoons chia seeds, plus more for serving (optional)
- 1 tablespoon hemp seeds
- ¼ cup chopped walnuts
- Nut butter, for serving (optional)

Directions:

Finely dice half the green apple and 1 Honeycrisp apple. Store in an airtight container with the lemon juice while you work on next steps.

Coarsely chop the remaining apples and the dates. Transfer to a food processor and add the cinnamon and nutmeg. Pulse several times to combine, then process for 2 to 3 minutes to purée. Stir the purée into the reserved diced apples. Stir in the chia seeds (if using), hemp seeds, and walnuts. Refrigerate for at least 1 hour before serving.

Serve as is or top with additional chia seeds and nut butter (if using).

Nutrition: Calories: 274; Fat: 8g; Carbs: 52g; Protein: 4g ; Fiber: 9g

4 **Pear and Polenta**

Preparation Time: 10 minutes

Cooking Time: 50 minutes

Serves 4

Ingredients:

- 5¼ cups water, divided, plus more as needed
- 1½ cups coarse cornmeal
- 3 tablespoons pure maple syrup
- 1 tablespoon molasses
- 1 teaspoon ground cinnamon
- 2 ripe pears, cored and diced

- 1 cup fresh cranberries
- 1 teaspoon chopped fresh rosemary leaves

Directions:

In an 8-quart pot over high heat, bring 5 cups of water to a simmer.

While whisking continuously to avoid clumping, slowly pour in the cornmeal. Cook, stirring often with a heavy spoon, for 30 minutes. The polenta should be thick and creamy.

While the polenta cooks, in a saucepan over medium heat, stir together the maple syrup, molasses, the remaining ¼ cup of water, and the cinnamon until combined. Bring to a simmer. Add the pears and cranberries. Cook for 10 minutes, stirring occasionally, until the pears are tender and start to brown. Remove from the heat. Stir in the rosemary and let the mixture sit for 5 minutes. If it is too thick, add another ¼ cup of water and return to the heat.

Top with the cranberry-pear mixture.

Nutrition: Calories: 282; Fat: 2g; Carbs: 65g; Protein: 4g; Fiber: 12g

5 <u>Blueberry Pecan Muffins</u>

<u>Preparation Time:</u> 20 minutes

<u>Cooking Time</u>: 30 minutes

<u>Servings</u>: Makes 12 muffins

<u>Ingredients:</u>

- 8 ounces (227 g) Medjool dates, pitted and chopped
- 1 cup plant-based milk
- 1 tablespoon freshly squeezed lemon juice
- 1 cup whole wheat flour

- ½ cup sorghum flour
- 1 cup millet flour
- 2 teaspoons baking powder
- 1 teaspoon ground cinnamon
- ½ teaspoon ground cardamom
- ½ teaspoon ground ginger
- 1 teaspoon lemon zest
- ½ cup unsweetened applesauce
- 1 cup fresh or frozen blueberries
- ½ cup chopped pecans

Directions:

Preheat the oven to 350ºF (180ºC). Line a 12-cup metal muffin pan with parchment-paper liners or use a silicone muffin pan.

In a small bowl, stir together the dates, milk, and lemon juice. Set aside.

In a medium bowl, whisk together the whole wheat, sorghum, and millet flours; baking powder; cinnamon; cardamom; ginger; and lemon zest to combine.

Pour the dates and soaking liquid into a high-speed blender. Blend until smooth. Add the applesauce and blend until combined.

Using a heavy spoon, fold the wet ingredients into the dry ingredients. Gently fold in the blueberries and pecans. Evenly spoon the batter into your muffin cups (they should be filled about three-quarters full).

Bake for 30 minutes, or until a toothpick inserted into the center of a muffin comes out clean. Let cool in the pan for 15 minutes before removing and transferring to a wire rack to cool.

Store in an airtight container at room temperature for up to 1 week or freeze for up to 3 months.

Nutrition (1 muffin): Calories: 192; Fat: 4g; Carbs: 37g; Protein: 4g; Fiber: 4g

Lunch

6 Pesto & White Bean Pasta

Preparation Time: 15 minutes

Cooking Time: 10 minutes

Servings: 4

Ingredients:

- 8 ounces rotini pasta, cooked according to the package directions, drained, and rinsed with cold water to cool
- 1½ cups canned cannellini beans or navy beans, drained and rinsed
- ½ cup Spinach Pesto
- 1 cup chopped tomato or red bell pepper

- ¼ red onion, finely diced
- ½ cup chopped pitted black olives

Directions:

Preparing the Ingredients

In a large bowl, combine the pasta, beans, and pesto. Toss to combine.

Add the tomato, red onion, and olives, tossing thoroughly. Store leftovers in an airtight container in the refrigerator for up to 1 week.

Nutrition: Calories: 544; Protein: 23g; Total fat: 17g; Saturated fat: 3g; Carbohydrates: 83g; Fiber: 13g

7 **Curried Lentils (Pressure cooker)**

Preparation Time: 6 minutes

Cooking Time: 20 minutes, High

Servings: 6-8

Ingredients:

- 1 tablespoon coconut oil
- 2 tablespoons mild curry powder
- 1 teaspoon ground ginger
- ½ teaspoon ground turmeric (optional)
- 1 cup dried green lentils or brown lentils
- 3 cups water

- 1 teaspoon freshly squeezed lime juice (optional)
- ½ teaspoon salt
- Freshly ground black pepper (optional)

Directions:

Preparing the Ingredients. On your electric pressure cooker, select Sauté. Add the coconut oil, curry powder, ginger, and turmeric (if using) and toss to toast for 1 minute. Add the lentils and toss with the spices. Add the water. Cancel Sauté.

High pressure for 20 minutes. Close and lock the lid, ensuring the pressure valve is sealed, then select High Pressure and set the time for 20 minutes.

Pressure Release. Once the cook time is complete, let the pressure release naturally, about 30 minutes.

Once all the pressure has released, carefully unlock and remove the lid. Stir in the lime juice (if using). Season with the salt and pepper, if you like.

Nutrition: Calories: 212; Total fat: 5g; Protein: 13g; Sodium: 2mg; Fiber: 16g

8 **Pesto Pearled Barley**

Preparation Time: 1 minutes

Cooking Time: 50 minutes

Servings: 4

Ingredients:

- 1 cup dried barley
- 2½ cups vegetable broth
- ½ cup Parm-y Kale Pesto

Directions:

In a medium saucepan, combine the barley and broth, then bring to boil.

Cover, reduce the heat to low, and simmer for about 45 minutes until tender.

Remove from the stove and let it stand for 5 minutes.

Finish and Serve

Fluff the barley, then gently fold in the pesto.

Scoop about ¾ cup into each of 4 single-compartment storage containers. Let it cool before sealing the lids.

Nutrition: Calories: 237; Fat: 6g; Protein: 9g; Carbohydrates: 40g; Fiber: 11g; Sugar: 2g; Sodium: 365mg

9 Creamy Cheese Asparagus

Preparation Time: 10 minutes

Cooking Time: 20 minutes

Servings: 2

Ingredients:

- 1 lb. asparagus, wash and trim off the ends
- 1 cup mozzarella cheese, shredded
- 1/2 cup asiago cheese, grated
- 1 tablespoon Italian seasoning
- 1 cup heavy whipping cream
- Pepper
- Salt

Directions:

Preheat the oven to 400F.

Spray baking dish with cooking spray and set aside

Place asparagus into the prepared baking dish

In a small bowl, whisk together heavy cream, asiago cheese, Italian seasoning, pepper and salt.

Pour heavy cream mixture over the asparagus.

Sprinkle with shredded mozzarella cheese

Bake in preheated oven for 18 minutes

Nutrition: Calories: 163; Carbs: 2g; Fat: 4g; Protein: 8g

10   Quinoa and Rice Stuffed Peppers (oven-baked)

Preparation Time: 10-30 minutes

Cooking Time: 35 minutes

Servings: 8

Ingredients:

- 3/4 cup long-grain rice
- 8 bell peppers (any color)
- 2 Tablespoon olive oil
- 1 onion finely diced
- 2 cloves chopped garlic

- 1 can (11 oz) crushed tomatoes
- 1 teaspoon cumin
- 1 teaspoon coriander
- 4 Tablespoon ground walnuts
- 2 cups cooked quinoa
- 4 Tablespoon chopped parsley
- Salt and ground black pepper to taste

Directions:

Preheat oven to 400 F/200 C.

Boil rice and drain in a colander.

Cut the top stem section of the pepper off, remove the remaining pith and seeds, rinse peppers.

Heat oil in a large frying skillet, and sauté onion and garlic until soft.

Add tomatoes, cumin, ground almonds, salt, pepper, and coriander; stir well and simmer for 2 minutes stirring constantly.

Remove from the heat and add the rice, quinoa, and parsley; stir well.

Taste and adjust salt and pepper.

Fill the peppers with a mixture, and place peppers cut side-up in a baking dish; drizzle with little oil.

Bake for 15 minutes.

Serve warm.

Nutrition: Calories: 335.69; Calories from Fat: 83.63; Total Fat: 9.58g; Saturated Fat: 1.2g;

11   **Quinoa and Lentils with Crushed Tomato**

Preparation Time: 10-30 minutes

Cooking Time: 35 minutes

Servings: 4

Ingredients:

- 4 Tablespoon olive oil
- 1 medium onion, diced

- 2 garlic clove, minced
- Salt and ground black pepper to taste
- 1 can (15 oz) tomatoes crushed
- 1 cup vegetable broth
- 1/2 cup quinoa, washed and drained
- 1 cup cooked lentils
- 1 teaspoon chili powder
- 1 teaspoon cumin

Directions:

Heat oil in a pot and sauté the onion and garlic with the pinch of salt until soft.

Pour reserved tomatoes and vegetable broth, bring to boil, and stir well.

Stir in the quinoa, cover and cook for 15 minutes; stir occasionally.

Add in lentils, chili powder, and cumin; cook for further 5 minutes.

Taste and adjust seasonings.

Serve immediately.

Keep refrigerated in a covered container for 4 - 5 days.

Nutrition: Calories: 397.45; Saturated Fat: 2.14g; Calories from Fat: 138.18; Total Fat: 15.61g

12   Silk Tofu Penne with Spinach

Preparation Time: 10-30 minutes

Cooking Time: 25 minutes

Servings: 4

Ingredients:

- 1 lb. penne, uncooked
- oz of frozen spinach, thawed
- 1 cup silken tofu mashed
- 1/2 cup soy milk (unsweetened)
- 1/2 cup vegetable broth
- 1 Tablespoon white wine vinegar
- 1/2 teaspoon Italian seasoning
- Salt and ground pepper to taste

Directions:

Cook penne pasta; rinse and drain in a colander.

Drain spinach well.

Place spinach with all remaining Ingredients: in a blender and beat until smooth.

Pour the spinach mixture over pasta.

Taste and adjust the salt and pepper.

Store pasta in an airtight container in the refrigerator for 3 to 5 days.

Nutrition: Calories: 492.8; Calories from Fat: 27.06; Total Fat: 3.07g; Saturated Fat: 0.38g

Snacks

13 <u>Banana Peanut Butter Yogurt Bowl</u>

<u>*Preparation Time*</u>: 5 minutes

<u>*Cooking Time*</u>: 0 minutes

<u>*Servings:*</u> 4

<u>*Ingredients:*</u>

- 1 teaspoon nutmeg
- ¼ Creamy peanut butter
- 2 medium-sized sliced bananas
- 4 cups vanilla flavor
- Soy yogurt

<u>*Directions:*</u>

Divide the yogurt among four bowls and top with the slices of bananas. Soften the microwave in the microwave for forty seconds and then put one tablespoon into each bowl, then garnish with the nutmeg and flaxseed meal.

Nutrition: Calories 292 Fat 15g Carbs 24g Protein 29g Fiber 3g

14   **Peanut Butter Fudge**

Preparation Time: 30 minutes

Cooking Time: 0 minutes

Servings: 20

Ingredients:

- 1 teaspoon vanilla extract
- 3 tablespoons maple syrup
- ½ cup coconut oil
- 1 cup creamy peanut butter
- 2 cups coconut flakes, unsweetened

Directions:

Use spray oil on an eight-inch square pan. Cream the shredded coconut in a food processor until it forms a buttery substance. Put the coconut butter into a bowl and blend in the coconut oil and peanut butter. Then add in the vanilla and mix once more. Spoon the mix into the pan and let it set.

Nutrition: Calories: 164; Protein: 4g; Fiber: 2g; Carbs: 5g; Fat: 16g

15   **Roasted Chickpeas**

Preparation Time: 5 minutes

Cooking Time: 30 minutes

Servings: 4

Ingredients:

- 1 (14.5-ounce) can chickpeas, drained but not rinsed
- 1 teaspoon extra-virgin olive oil or 2 teaspoons reserved chickpea brine
- 1 teaspoon smoked paprika
- 1 teaspoon garlic powder

Directions:

Preheat the oven to 425ºF. Line a baking sheet with parchment paper.

After draining the chickpeas, pat dry with a paper towel. Transfer to a medium bowl. Add the olive oil, paprika, and garlic powder. Using a wooden spoon or your hands, toss gently to coat.

Spread the chickpeas out on the prepared baking sheet in a single layer. Roast for 30 minutes, rotating the baking sheet after 15 minutes.

Turn the oven off, open the oven door about five inches, and allow the chickpeas to cool in the oven. Transfer all of the chickpeas into a glass pint jar or divide evenly among 4 (4-ounce) jelly jars. Cool completely before closing tightly with lids.

Nutrition: Calories: 157 Total fat: 3g Carbohydrates: 28g Fiber: 6g Protein: 6g

16   Tamari Almonds

Preparation Time: 5 minutes

Cooking Time: 15 minutes

Servings: 8

Ingredients:

- 1 pound raw almonds
- 3 tablespoons tamari or soy sauce
- 2 tablespoons extra-virgin olive oil

- 1 tablespoon nutritional yeast
- 1 to 2 teaspoons chili powder, to taste

Directions:

Preheat the oven to 400ºF. Line a baking sheet with parchment paper.

In a medium bowl, combine the almonds, tamari, and olive oil until well coated. Spread the almonds on the prepared baking sheet and roast for 10 to 15 minutes until browned.

Cool for 10 minutes, then season with the nutritional yeast and chili powder.

Transfer to a glass jar and close tightly with a lid.

Nutrition: Calories: 364 Total fat: 32g Carbohydrates: 13g Fiber: 6g Protein: 13g

17   Taco Pita Pizzas

Preparation Time: 5 minutes

Cooking Time: 7 minutes

Servings: 4

Ingredients:

- 4 sandwich-size pita bread pieces or Sandwich Thins
- 1 cup vegetarian refried beans
- 1 cup pizza sauce
- 1 cup chopped mushrooms
- 1 teaspoon minced jalapeño (optional)

Directions:

Preheat the oven to 400ºF. Line a large baking sheet with parchment paper.

Assemble 4 pizzas: On each pita, spread about ¼ cup of refried beans. Pour ¼ cup of pizza sauce over the beans and spread evenly. Add ¼ cup of mushrooms. Sprinkle ¼ teaspoon of minced jalapeño (if using) over the mushrooms.

Place the pizzas on the prepared baking sheet and bake for 7 minutes.

Cool completely before placing each pizza in a freezer-safe plastic bag, or store together in one large airtight, freezer-safe container with parchment paper between the pizzas.

Nutrition: Calories: 148; Total fat: 2g; Carbohydrates: 29g; Fiber: 5g; Protein: 6g

18   Risotto Bites

Preparation Time: 15 minutes

Cooking Time: 20 minutes

Servings: 12 bites

Ingredients:

- ½ cup panko bread crumbs
- 1 teaspoon paprika
- 1 teaspoon chipotle powder or ground cayenne pepper
- 1½ cups cold Green Pea Risotto
- Nonstick cooking spray

Directions:

Preheat the oven to 425ºF. Line a baking sheet with parchment paper.

On a large plate, combine the panko, paprika, and chipotle powder. Set aside.

Roll 2 tablespoons of the risotto into a ball. Gently roll in the bread crumbs and place on the prepared baking sheet. Repeat to make a total of 12 balls.

Spritz the tops of the risotto bites with nonstick cooking spray and bake for 15 to 20 minutes, until they begin to brown.

Cool completely before storing in a large airtight container in a single layer (add a piece of parchment paper for a second layer) or in a plastic freezer bag.

Nutrition: Calories: 100 Total fat: 2g Carbohydrates: 17g Fiber: 5g Protein: 6g

19   **Healthy Protein Bars**

Preparation Time: 19 minutes

Cooking Time: 0 minutes

Servings: 12 balls

Ingredients:

- 1 large banana
- 1 cup of rolled oats
- 1 serving of vegan vanilla protein powder

Directions:

Using your food processor, blend the protein powder, and rolled oats.

Blend them for 1 minute until you have a semi-coarse mixture. The oats should be slightly chopped, but not powdered.

Add the banana and form a pliable and coarse dough.

Shape into either balls or small bars and store them in a container.

Eat one and store the rest in an airtight container in the refrigerator!

Nutrition: Fat 0.7 g Carbohydrates 8 g Protein- 2.7 g Calories: 47

20   Quick Peanut Butter Bars

Preparation Time: 10 minutes

Cooking Time: 0 minutes

Servings: 10

Ingredients:

- 20 soft-pitted Medjool dates
- 1 cup of raw almonds
- 1 ¼ cup of crushed pretzels
- 1/3 cup of natural peanut butter

Directions:

Transfer your almonds to a food processor and mix them until they are broken.

Add the peanut butter and the dates. Blend them until you have a thick dough

Crush the pretzels and put them in the processor. Pulse enough to mix them with the rest of the ingredients. You can also give them a good stir with a spoon.

Take a small, square pan and line it with parchment paper. Press the dough onto the pan, flattening it with your hands or a spoon.

Put it in the freezer for about 2 hours or in the fridge for about 4 hours.

Once it is fully set, cut it into bars. Store them and enjoy them when you are hungry. Just remember to store them in a sealed container.

Nutrition: Calories: 343 Fat 23 g Carbohydrates 33 g Protein 5 g

21   Hummus without Oil

Preparation Time: 5 minutes

Cooking Time: 0 minutes

Servings: 6

Ingredients:

- 2 tablespoons of lemon juice
- 1 15-ounce can of chickpeas
- 2 tablespoons of tahini
- 1-2 freshly chopped/minced garlic cloves
- Red pepper hummus
- 2 tablespoons of almond milk pepper

Directions:

Wash with running water the chickpeas and put them in a high-speed blender with garlic. Blend them until they break into fine pieces.

Add the other ingredients and blend everything until you have a smooth paste. Add some water if you want a less thick consistency.

Your homemade hummus dip is ready to be served with eatables

Nutrition: Calories: 202 Fat 3 g Carbohydrates 35 g Protein 11 g

Salads

22   Caramelized Onion And Beet Salad

Preparation Time: 10 minutes

Cooking Time: 40 minutes

Servings: 4

Ingredients:

- 3 medium golden beets
- 2 cups sliced sweet or Vidalia onions
- 1 teaspoon extra-virgin olive oil or no-beef broth
- Pinch baking soda
- ¼ to ½ teaspoon salt, to taste
- 2 tablespoons unseasoned rice vinegar, white wine vinegar, or balsamic vinegar

Directions:

Cut the greens off the beets, and scrub the beets.

In a large pot, place a steamer basket and fill the pot with 2 inches of water.

Add the beets, bring to boil, then reduce the heat to medium, cover, and steam for about 35 minutes until you can easily pierce the middle of the beets with a knife.

Meanwhile, in a large, dry skillet over medium heat, sauté the onions for 5 minutes while stirring frequently.

Add the olive oil and baking soda, then continuing cooking for 5 more minutes while stirring frequently. Stir in the salt before removing from the heat. Transfer to a large bowl and set aside.

Finish and Serve

When the beets have cooked through, drain and cool until easy to handle. Rub the beets in a paper towel to easily remove the skins. Cut into wedges, and transfer to the bowl with the onions. Drizzle the vinegar over everything and toss well.

Divide the beets evenly among 4 wide-mouth jars or storage containers. Let it cool before sealing the lids.

Nutrition: Calories: 104; Fat: 2g; Protein: 3g; Carbohydrates: 20g; Fiber: 4g; Sugar: 14g; Sodium: 303mg

23   Warm Lentil Salad with Red Wine Vinaigrette

Preparation Time: 10 minutes

Cooking Time: 50 minutes

Servings: 4

Ingredients:

- 1 teaspoon extra-virgin olive oil plus ¼ cup, divided, or 1 tablespoon vegetable broth or water
- 1 small onion, diced
- 1 garlic clove, minced
- 1 carrot, diced
- 1 cup lentils
- 1 tablespoon dried basil
- 1 tablespoon dried oregano
- 1 tablespoon red wine or balsamic vinegar (optional)
- 2 cups water
- ¼ cup red wine vinegar or balsamic vinegar
- 1 teaspoon sea salt
- 2 cups chopped Swiss chard

- 2 cups torn red leaf lettuce
- 4 tablespoons Cheesy Sprinkle

Directions:

Heat 1 teaspoon of the oil in a large pot on medium heat, then sauté the onion and garlic until they are translucent.

Add the carrot and sauté until it is slightly cooked. Stir in the lentils, basil, and oregano, then add the wine or balsamic vinegar (if using).

Pour the water into the pot and turn the heat up to high to bring to boil.

Turn the heat down to a simmer and let the lentils cook, uncovered, for 20-30 minutes until they are soft but not falling apart.

While the lentils are cooking, whisk together the red wine vinegar, olive oil, and salt in a small bowl and set aside. Once the lentils have cooked, drain any excess liquid and stir in most of the red wine vinegar dressing. Set a little bit of dressing aside. Add the Swiss chard to the pot and stir it into the lentils.

Leave the heat on low and cook, stirring, for at least 10 minutes.

Finish and Serve

Toss the lettuce with the remaining dressing. Place some lettuce on a plate, and top with the lentil mixture. Finish the plate off with a little cheesy sprinkle and enjoy.

Nutrition: Calories: 387; Total fat: 17g; Carbs: 42g; Fiber: 19g; Protein: 18g

24   Red Bean And Corn Salad

Preparation Time: 15 minutes

Cooking Time: 0 minutes

Servings: 4

Ingredients:

- ¼ cup Cashew Cream or other salad dressing
- 1 teaspoon chili powder
- 2 (14.5-ounce) cans kidney beans, rinsed and drained

- 2 cups frozen corn, thawed, or 2 cups canned corn, drained
- 1 cup cooked farro, barley, or rice (optional)
- 8 cups chopped romaine lettuce

Directions:

Line up 4 wide-mouth glass quart jars.

In a small bowl, whisk the cream and chili powder. Pour 1 tablespoon of cream into each jar. In each jar, add ¾ cup kidney beans, ½ cup corn, ¼ cup cooked farro (if using), and 2 cups romaine, punching it down to fit it into the jar. Close the lids tightly.

Nutrients: Calories: 303; Fat: 9g; Protein: 14g; Carbohydrates: 45g; Fiber: 15g; Sugar: 6g; Sodium: 654mg

25   Tabbouleh Salad

Preparation Time: 15 minutes

Cooking Time: 10 minutes

Servings: 4

Ingredients:

- 1 cup whole-wheat couscous
- 1 cup boiling water
- Zest and juice of 1 lemon
- 1 garlic clove, pressed
- Pinch sea salt
- 1 tablespoon extra-virgin olive oil, or flaxseed oil (optional)
- ½ cucumber, diced small
- 1 tomato, diced small
- 1 cup fresh parsley, chopped
- ¼ cup fresh mint, finely chopped
- 2 scallions, finely chopped
- 4 tablespoons sunflower seeds (optional)

Directions:

Preparing the Ingredients.

Put the couscous in a medium bowl, and cover with boiling water until all the grains are submerged. Cover the bowl with a plate or wrap. Set aside.

Put the lemon zest and juice in a large salad bowl, then stir in the garlic, salt, and the olive oil (if using).

Put the cucumber, tomato, parsley, mint, and scallions in the bowl, and toss them to coat with the dressing. Take the plate off the couscous and fluff with a fork.

Finish and Serve

Add the cooked couscous to the vegetables, then toss to combine.

Serve topped with the sunflower seeds (if using).

Nutrition: Calories: 304; Total fat: 11g; Carbs: 44g; Fiber: 6g; Protein: 10g

26   **Tuscan White Bean Salad**

Preparation Time: 10 minutes

Cooking Time: 30 minutes (marinating time)

Servings: 2

Ingredients:

THE DRESSING :

- 1 tablespoon extra-virgin olive oil
- 2 tablespoons balsamic vinegar
- 1 teaspoon minced fresh chives, or scallions
- 1 garlic clove, pressed or minced
- 1 tablespoon fresh rosemary, chopped, or 1 teaspoon dried
- 1 tablespoon fresh oregano, chopped, or 1 teaspoon dried
- Pinch sea salt

THE SALAD:

- 1 (14-ounce) can cannellini beans, drained and rinsed, or 1½ cups cooked
- 6 mushrooms, thinly sliced

- 1 zucchini, diced
- 2 carrots, diced
- 2 tablespoons fresh basil, chopped

Directions:

Preparing the Ingredients

Make the dressing by whisking all the dressing ingredients together in a large bowl.

Toss all the salad ingredients with the dressing.

Finish and Serve

For the best flavor, put the salad in a sealed container, shake it vigorously, then leave to marinate for 15-30 minutes.

Nutrition: Calories: 360; Total fat: 8g; Carbs: 68g; Fiber: 15g; Protein: 18g

27   **<u>Moroccan Aubergine Salad</u>**

<u>Preparation Time:</u> 30 minutes

<u>Cooking Time</u>: 15 minutes

<u>Servings:</u> 2

<u>Ingredients:</u>

- 1 teaspoon extra-virgin olive oil
- 1 eggplant, diced
- ½ teaspoon ground cumin
- ½ teaspoon ground ginger
- ¼ teaspoon turmeric
- ¼ teaspoon ground nutmeg
- Pinch sea salt
- 1 lemon, half zested and juiced, half cut into wedges
- 2 tablespoons capers
- 1 tablespoon chopped green olives
- 1 garlic clove, pressed
- Handful fresh mint, finely chopped
- 2 cups spinach, chopped

Directions:

Heat the oil in a large skillet on medium heat, then sauté the eggplant. Once it has softened slightly, stir in the cumin, ginger, turmeric, nutmeg, and salt. Cook until the eggplant is very soft.

Add the lemon zest and juice, capers, olives, garlic, and mint. Sauté for another minute or two to blend the flavors. Put a handful of spinach on each plate, and spoon the eggplant mixture on top.

Serve with a wedge of lemon to squeeze the fresh juice over the greens.

To tenderize the eggplant and reduce some of its naturally occurring bitter taste, you can sweat the eggplant by salting it.

After dicing the eggplant, sprinkle it with salt and let it sit in a colander for about 30 minutes. Rinse the eggplant to remove the salt, then continue with the recipe as written.

Nutrition: Calories: 97; Total fat: 4g; Carbs: 16g; Fiber: 8g; Protein: 4g

Side Dishes

28   Broccoli and Black Bean Chili

Preparation Time: 15 minutes

Cooking Time: 15 minutes

Servings: 2

Ingredients:

- ½ tablespoon coconut oil
- 1 cup broccoli
- 1 cup chopped red onions
- ½ tablespoon paprika
- 1/2 teaspoon salt
- ¼ cup tomatoes
- 1 cup black beans drained, rinsed
- ¼ chopped green chills
- ½ cup of water

Directions:

In the Instant Pot, select Sauté; adjust to normal. Heat coconut oil in Instant Pot. Add broccoli, onions, paprika, and salt; cook

8 to 10 minutes, stirring occasionally, until thoroughly cooked. Select Cancel.

Stir in tomatoes, black beans, chills, and water. Secure lid set pressure valve to Sealing. Select Manual, cook on High pressure 5 minutes. Select Cancel. Keep the pressure valve in the Sealing position to release pressure naturally.

Nutrition: Calories: 408; Total Fat: 5. 3g; Saturated Fat: 3. 4g; Cholesterol: 0mg; Sodium: 607mg; Total Carbohydrate: 70. 7g; Dietary Fiber: 18. 1g; Total Sugars: 6g; Protein: 23. 3g

29   **Vegetarian Chili**

Preparation Time: 15 minutes

Cooking Time: 20 minutes

Servings: 2

Ingredients:

- 1 tablespoon avocado oil
- ½ teaspoon garlic powder
- 1 cup chopped onion
- ½ cup chopped carrots

- ¼ cup chopped green bell pepper
- ¼ cup chopped red bell pepper
- 1 tablespoon chili powder
- ½ cup chopped fresh mushrooms
- ½ cup whole peeled tomatoes with liquid, chopped
- ¼ cup black beans
- ¼ cup kidney beans
- ¼ cup pinto beans
- ¼ cup whole kernel corn
- ½ tablespoon cumin seed
- 1/2 tablespoons dried basil
- 1/2 tablespoon garlic minced

Directions:

Select the Sauté setting on the Instant Pot, add avocado oil, cook and stir the garlic minced, onions, and carrots in the Instant Pot until tender. Mix in the green bell pepper, red bell pepper, and chili powder. Season with chili powder. Continue cooking for 2 minutes, or until the peppers are tender.

Mix the mushrooms into the Instant pot. Stir in the tomatoes with liquid, black beans, kidney beans, pinto beans, and corn. Season with cumin seed, basil, and garlic powder.

Select Pressure Cook or Manual, and adjust the pressure to High and the time to 12 minutes. After cooking, let the pressure release naturally for 10 minutes, then quickly release any remaining pressure.

Nutrition: Calories: 348; Total Fat: 3. 3g; Saturated Fat: 0. 6g; Cholesterol: 0mg; Sodium: 77mg; Total Carbohydrate: 65g; Dietary Fiber: 16. 5g; Total Sugars: 9. 5g; Protein: 19. 1g

30 **Coconut Curry Chili**

Preparation Time: 15 minutes

Cooking Time: 30 minutes

Servings: 2

Ingredients:

- 1 cup tomatoes
- 2 cups of water
- 1 tablespoon minced garlic

- ½ cup garbanzo beans
- ½ cup red kidney beans
- 1/2 cup chopped zucchini
- ¼ cup mango
- 1 1/2 tablespoons curry powder
- 1cup onions, chopped
- Salt and ground black pepper to taste
- ½ cup of coconut milk

Directions:

In the Instant Pot, add all ingredients like tomatoes, water, garlic, garbanzo beans, kidney beans, zucchini, mango, curry powder, onions, salt, and black pepper.

Select Pressure Cook or Manual, and adjust the pressure to High and the time to 12 minutes. After cooking, let the pressure release naturally for 10 minutes, then quickly release any remaining pressure. Stir coconut milk. Serve.

Nutrition: Calories: 548; Total Fat: 18. 6g; Saturated Fat: 13. 2g; Cholesterol: 0mg; Sodium: 46mg; Total Carbohydrate: 78g; Dietary Fiber: 21. 1g; Total Sugars: 16. 6g; Protein: 24g

31   **Spicy Butternut Squash Chili**

Preparation Time: 15 minutes

Cooking Time: 30 minutes

Servings: 2

Ingredients:

- ½ teaspoon crushed red pepper flakes, or to taste
- 1 teaspoon garlic powder
- ½ large onion, diced
- 1 green bell pepper, chopped
- 1 red bell pepper, chopped
- ½ cup kidney beans
- ½ cup black beans
- ½ cup pinto beans,
- 1 cup tomato paste
- 2 tomatoes, diced
- ½ cup butter squash diced
- ½ cup green peas
- ½ teaspoons chili powder
- 1 teaspoon cumin

- Salt and pepper

Directions:

In the Instant Pot, combine red pepper flakes, garlic powder, onion, kidney beans, black beans, pinto beans, tomato paste, diced tomatoes, and butter squash.

Add the green and red bell pepper and water and cook for 5 minutes. Season with chili powder, cumin, and salt.

Stir the green peas, salt, and pepper into the Instant pot. Select Pressure Cook or Manual, and adjust the pressure to High and the time to 12 minutes. After cooking, let the pressure release naturally for 10 minutes, then quickly release any remaining pressure.

Serve and enjoy.

Nutrition: Calories: 620; Total Fat: 2. 9g; Saturated Fat: 0. 6g; Cholesterol: 0mg; Sodium: 37mg; Total Carbohydrate: 117. 2g; Dietary Fiber: 29. 3g; Total Sugars: 16. 1g; Protein: 37g

32   **Creamy White Beans and Chickpeas Chili**

Preparation Time: 05 minutes

Cooking Time: 35 minutes

Servings: 2

Ingredients:

- 1 teaspoon coconut oil
- 1 onion finely diced
- ½ teaspoon garlic powder
- 2 cups vegetable broth
- ½ cup chickpeas
- ½ cup navy beans
- ½ tablespoon chili powder
- ½ cumin powder
- ½ teaspoon kosher salt
- ¼ teaspoon black pepper
- 1/2 cup butter
- 3 tablespoon coconut flour
- 1 cup coconut milk warmed
- ¼ cup coconut cream

- ½ tablespoon lime juice

Directions:

Add coconut oil to the Instant Pot. Using the display panel select the Sauté function.

When oil gets hot, add onion to the pot and sauté until soft, 3-4 minutes. Add garlic powder and cook for 1-2 minutes more.

Add broth to the pot and deglaze by using a wooden spoon to scrape the brown bits from the bottom of the pot.

Add chickpeas, beans, chili and cumin powder, salt, and pepper, and stir to combine.

Turn the pot off by selecting Cancel, then secure the lid, making sure the vent is closed.

Using the display panel select the Manual or Pressure Cook function. Use the + /- keys and program the Instant Pot for 15 minutes.

When the time is up, let the pressure naturally release for 10 minutes, then quickly release the remaining pressure.

In a medium bowl, melt butter, then whisk in flour until well combined. Stir into the pot and simmer 3-5 minutes until thickened, returning to Sauté   mode as needed.

Stir in coconut milk, coconut cream, and lime juice. Adjust seasonings.

Nutrition: Calories: 1086; Total Fat: 71. 3g; Saturated Fat: 47. 6g; Cholesterol: 122mg; Sodium: 1764mg; Total Carbohydrate: 86. 3g; Dietary Fiber: 32. 3g; Total Sugars: 14. 5g; Protein: 32. 1g

33   Potato Chili

Preparation Time: 10 minutes

Cooking Time: 25 minutes

Servings: 2

Ingredients:

- ½ teaspoon olive oil
- ½ cup onion chopped
- ½ teaspoon garlic powder
- ½ teaspoon chili powder

- ½ teaspoon ground cumin
- 1 cup diced tomatoes
- ½ cup black beans rinsed and drained
- 1 medium red bell pepper seeded and diced
- 1 medium potato peeled and diced
- 1 teaspoon kosher salt
- ¼ cup frozen corn kernels

Directions:

Select Sauté and add the olive oil to the Instant Pot. Add the onions and garlic powder. Sauté for 2 minutes, or until the garlic powder is fragrant and the onion is soft and translucent.

Add the chili powder and ground cumin, followed by the tomatoes, black beans, red bell pepper, potato, corn, and salt. Stir well.

Cover, lock the lid and flip the steam release handle to the Sealing position. Select Pressure Cook High and set the cooking time for 15 minutes. When the cooking time is complete, allow the pressure to release naturally for about 20 minutes.

Remove the lid and ladle the chili into serving bowls. Serve hot.

Nutrition: Calories: 207; Total Fat: 2. 1g; Saturated Fat: 0. 3g; Cholesterol: 0mg; Sodium: 1207mg; Total Carbohydrate: 41. 4g; Dietary Fiber: 8. 8g; Total Sugars: 7. 7g; Protein: 8. 2g

34   **Beans Baby Potato Curry**

Preparation Time: 10 minutes

Cooking Time: 30 minutes

Servings: 2

Ingredients:

- 1 small onion, chopped
- ½ teaspoon garlic, chopped finely
- 1 cup baby potatoes
- ½ tablespoon curry powder
- 2 cups of water
- ½ cup pinto beans
- ½ cup milk
- ½ tablespoon honey
- Salt & pepper to taste
- ½ teaspoon chili pepper flakes
- 1 tablespoon arrowroot powder

Directions:

Set your Instant Pot to Sauté. Once hot, add a few drops of water and cook the onions until translucent, then add the garlic and cook for one minute longer. Press the Keep Warm/Cancel button.

Add everything to the Instant Pot except the arrowroot powder.

Set the Instant Pot to 20 minutes on Manual High pressure and allow the pressure to release naturally after this time.

Press Keep Warm/Cancel, remove the lid, and press Sauté. Put the arrowroot into a small bowl or cup and mix into it a few tablespoons of water to make a thickness but pour slurry. Pour it into the Instant Pot stirring as you go.

Add salt and pepper to taste then cook for about 5 minutes until they are tender and the gravy has thickened.

Serve immediately.

Nutrition: Calories: 342; Total Fat: 2. 3g; Saturated Fat: 1g; Cholesterol: 5mg; Sodium: 58mg; Total Carbohydrate: 67. 2g; Dietary Fiber: 12. 1g; Total Sugars: 10g; Protein: 14. 2g

35   Butter Tofu with Soy Bean and Chickpeas

Preparation Time: 10 minutes

Cooking Time: 30 minutes

Servings: 2

Ingredients:

- 2 large ripe tomatoes
- ½ teaspoon garlic powder
- ½ teaspoon ginger powder
- ½ tablespoon hot green chili
- 1 cup of water
- ¼ teaspoon garam masala
- 1/8 teaspoon paprika
- ¼ teaspoon salt
- ¼ cup of soybeans
- ½ cup chickpeas
- ½ teaspoon honey
- ½ cup coconut cream
- Cilantro for garnish

Directions:

Blend the tomatoes, garlic powder, ginger powder, hot green chili with water until smooth.

Add pureed tomato mixture to the Instant Pot. Add soybeans, chickpeas, spices, and salt. Close the lid and cook on Manual for 8 to 10 minutes. Quick-release after 10 minutes.

Start the Instant Pot on Sauté. Add the coconut cream, Garam masala, honey, and mix in. Bring to a boil, taste, and adjust salt. Add more paprika and salt if needed.

Serve with cilantro garnishing

Nutrition: Calories: 242; Total Fat: 1. 3g; Saturated Fat: 1. 5g; Cholesterol: 5mg; Sodium: 38mg; Total Carbohydrate: 47. 2g; Dietary Fiber: 10. 1g; Total Sugars: 10g; Protein: 14. 2g.

Dinner

36   <u>Mashed Potatoes</u>

<u>*Preparation Time*</u>: 10 minutes

<u>*Cooking Time:*</u> 12 minutes

<u>*Servings:*</u> 2

<u>*Ingredients:*</u>

- 4 potatoes, halved
- 1/4 tablespoons chives, chopped
- 1 teaspoon minced garlic
- 3/4 teaspoon sea salt
- 2 tablespoons butter, unsalted
- 1/4 teaspoon ground black pepper

<u>*Directions:*</u>

Take a medium pot, place it over medium-high heat, add potatoes, cover with water and boil until cooked and tender.

When done, drain the potatoes, let them cool for 10 minutes, peel them and return them into the pot.

Mash the potatoes by using a hand mixer until fluffy, add remaining Ingredients: except for chives, and then stir until mixed.

Sprinkle chives over the top and then serve.

Nutrition: Calories: 365; Carbs: 10g; Fat: 5g; Protein: 67g

37 <u>Teriyaki Eggplant</u>

<u>*Preparation Time*</u>: 5 minutes

<u>*Cooking Time:*</u> 15 minutes

<u>*Servings:*</u> 2

<u>*Ingredients:*</u>

- 1/2 pound eggplant
- 1 green onion, chopped
- 1/2 teaspoon grated ginger
- 1/2 teaspoon minced garlic
- 1/3 cup soy sauce
- 1 tablespoon coconut sugar
- 1/2 tablespoon apple cider vinegar
- 1 tablespoon olive oil

Directions:

Prepare teriyaki sauce and for this, take a medium bowl, add ginger, garlic, soy sauce, vinegar, and sugar in it and then whisk until sugar has dissolved completely.

Cut eggplant into cubes, add them into teriyaki sauce, toss until well coated and marinate for 10 minutes.

When ready to cook, take a grill pan, place it over medium-high heat, grease it with oil, and when hot, add marinated eggplant.

Cook for 3 to 4 minutes per side until nicely browned and beginning to charred, drizzling with excess marinade frequently and transfer to a plate.

Sprinkle green onion on top of the eggplant and then serve.

Nutrition: Calories: 132; Carbs: 4g; Fat: 4g; Protein: 13g

38   **Scalloped Potatoes**

Preparation Time: 10 minutes

Cooking Time: 20 minutes

Servings: 2

Ingredients:

- 1 1/3 tablespoon flour
- 3 potatoes, peeled, sliced
- 2 green onions, sliced
- 6 tablespoons almond milk, unsweetened
- 3 tablespoons grated parmesan cheese
- 1/4 teaspoon salt
- 1/4 teaspoon ground black pepper
- 1/3 tablespoon butter, unsalted

Directions:

Switch on the oven, then set it to 350 degrees F and let it preheat.

Meanwhile, take a small saucepan, place it over medium-low heat, add butter and when it melts, stir in flour until smooth sauce comes together and then stir in salt and black pepper.

Whisk in milk until smooth, then remove the pan from heat and stir in 2 tablespoons cheese until melted.

Take a baking pan, grease it with oil, line its bottom with some of the potato slices, sprinkle with one-third of green onion, and cover with one-third of the sauce.

Create two more layers by using remaining potatoes, green onion, and sauce, and sprinkle cheese on top.

Cover baking pan with foil, bake for 20 minutes, uncover the pan and continue cooking for 5 minutes until the top has turned golden brown. Serve straight away.

Nutrition: Calories: 302; Carbs: 8g; Fat: 7g; Protein: 57g

39   Quinoa Enchiladas

Preparation Time: 10 minutes

Cooking Time: 40 minutes

Servings: 2

Ingredients:

- 1 tablespoon coconut oil
- 2 cloves garlic, minced
- 1 small yellow onion, chopped
- 3/4 pounds baby bella mushrooms, chopped
- 1/2 cup diced green chilis
- 1/2 teaspoon ground cumin
- 1/4 teaspoon sea salt (or to taste)
- 1 can organic, low sodium black beans or 1-1/2 cup cooked black beans
- 1-1/2 cup cooked quinoa
- 10 6-inch corn tortillas
- 1-1/4 cup organic, low sodium tomato or enchilada sauce

<u>*Directions:*</u>

Preheat oven to 350 degrees.

Heat coconut oil in a large pot over medium heat.

Sautee onion and garlic till onion is translucent (about 5-8 min) and add mushrooms and cook until liquid has been released and evaporated (another 5 min).

Add the chilis to the pot and give them a stir for 2 minutes.

Add the cumin, sea salt, black beans and quinoa, and continue heating the mixture until it's completely warm.

Spread a thin layer (1/2 cup) of marinara or enchilada sauce in the bottom of a casserole dish.

Place a third of a cup of quinoa mixture in the center of a corn tortilla and roll it up. Place the tortilla, seam down, in the casserole dish.

Repeat with all remaining tortillas and then cover them with 3/4 cup of additional sauce.

Bake for 25 minutes, and serve.

Nutrition: Calories: 201; Carbs: 4g; Fat: 4g; Protein: 11g

40   Mushroom Spinach Quiche

Preparation Time: 10 minutes

Cooking Time: 40 minutes

Servings: 4

Ingredients:

- 1 cup mozzarella cheese, shredded
- 1/2 teaspoon garlic powder
- 1/3 cup parmesan cheese shredded
- 1/2 cup water
- 1/2 cup heavy cream
- 6 large eggs
- 2 provolone cheese slices
- 8 oz can mushroom, sliced
- 10 oz frozen spinach, thawed and drained
- Pepper
- Salt

Directions:

Spray pie dish with cooking spray.

Spread spinach into the prepared pie dish.

Spread sliced mushrooms over the spinach.

Arrange cheese slices over the mushrooms.

Beat together eggs, water, and heavy cream. Stir in parmesan, pepper, garlic powder, and salt.

Pour egg mixture over spinach and mushrooms mixture.

Top with mozzarella cheese and bake at 350F for 40 minutes.

Cut into pieces and serve.

Nutrition: Calories: 198; Carbs: 6g; Fat: 4g; Protein: 16g

41   Sweet Potato and Black Bean Chili

Preparation Time: 15 minutes

Cooking Time: 40 minutes

Servings: 3

Ingredients:

- 1-1/2 cup dried black beans
- 4 cups sweet potato, diced into 3/4 inch cubes
- 1 tablespoon olive oil

- 1-1/2 cups chopped white or yellow onion
- 2 cloves garlic, minced
- 1 chipotle pepper in adobo, chopped finely
- 2 teaspoons cumin powder
- 1/2 teaspoon smoked paprika
- 1 tablespoon ground chili powder
- 1 14 or 15 ounce can of organic, diced tomatoes
- 1 can organic, low sodium black beans (or 1-1/2 cups cooked black beans)
- 2 cups low sodium vegetable broth.
- Sea salt to taste

Directions:

Heat the tablespoon of oil in a dutch oven or a large pot.

Sauté the onion for a few minutes, then add the sweet potato and garlic and keep sautéing until the onions are soft for about 8-10 minutes.

Add the chili in adobo, the cumin, the chili powder, and the smoked paprika and eat until the spices are very fragrant.

Add the tomatoes, black beans, and vegetable broth.

When broth is bubbling, reduce to a simmer and cook for approximately 25-30 minutes, or until the sweet potatoes are tender.

Add more broth as needed, and season to taste with salt.

Nutrition: Calories: 232; Carbs: 4g; Fat: 9g; Protein: 13g

42   Baked Zucchini with Herbs

Preparation Time: 10 minutes

Cooking Time: 40 minutes

Servings: 2

Ingredients:

- 2-1/2 lbs. zucchini, cut into quarters
- 1/3 cup parsley, chopped
- 1 teaspoon dried basil
- 1/2 cup parmesan cheese, shredded
- 6 garlic cloves, crushed
- 10 oz cherry tomatoes cut in half
- 1/2 teaspoon black pepper
- 3/4 teaspoon salt

Directions:

Preheat the oven to 350F.

Spray baking dish with cooking spray and set aside.

Mix all Ingredients: except parsley into the large mixing bowl and stir well to combine.

Pour egg mixture into the prepared baking dish.

Bake in preheated oven for 35 minutes.

Garnish with parsley and serve

Nutrition: Calories: 272; Carbs: 8g; Fat: 6g; Protein: 10g

43   **Creamy Broccoli Soup**

Preparation Time: 15 minutes

Cooking Time: 30 minutes

Servings: 4

Ingredients:

- 4 cup broccoli florets
- 1/2 teaspoon ground nutmeg

- 1 small avocado, peel and sliced
- 2 cups vegetable broth

Directions:

Add broth into the pot and bring to simmer over medium-high heat.

Add broccoli into the pot and cook for 8 minutes or until tender.

Reduce heat to low and add avocado and nutmeg.

Whisk well and cook for 4 minutes.

Using blender, puree the soup until smooth.

Serve and enjoy.

Nutrition: Calories: 159; Carbs: 4g; Fat: 4g; Protein: 11g

44   Healthy Brussels Sprout

Preparation Time: 10 minutes

Cooking Time: 5 minutes

Servings: 2

Ingredients:

- 6 Brussels sprouts, trimmed and cut in half
- 1 tablespoon parmesan cheese, grated
- 1 teaspoon olive oil
- 1/2 teaspoon apple cider vine gar
- 1/8 teaspoon black pepper
- Pinch of salt

Directions:

Add Brussels sprouts, olive oil, apple cider vinegar, black pepper, and salt into the mixing bowl and toss well.

Sprinkle parmesan cheese and mix well.

Serve and enjoy

Nutrition: Calories: 242; Carbs: 2g; Fat: 4g; Protein: 9g

45   Cabbage Zucchini Salad

Preparation Time: 5 minutes

Cooking Time: 10 minutes

Servings: 3

Ingredients:

- 1 medium zucchini, spiralized
- 1 teaspoon stevia
- 1/3 cup rice vinegar
- 3/4 cup olive oil
- 1 cup almonds, sliced
- 1 cup sunflower seeds shelled
- 1 lb. cabbage, shredded

Directions:

Chop spiralized zucchini into small pieces and set aside.

In large mixing bowl, combine together cabbage, almonds, and sunflower seeds

Stir in zucchini

In a small bowl, mix together oil, stevia, and vinegar. Whisk well and pour over vegetables.

Toss salad well and place in refrigerator for 2 hours

Serve and enjoy

Nutrition: Calories: 211; Carbs: 2g; Fat: 3g; Protein: 9g

Dessert

46   Chocolate Strawberry Shake

Preparation Time: 5 minutes

Cooking Time: 0 minutes

Servings: 2

Ingredients:

- 2 cups almond milk, unsweetened
- 4 bananas, peeled, frozen
- 4 tablespoons cocoa powder
- 2 cups strawberries, frozen

Directions:

Place all the ingredients into the jar of a high-speed food processor or blender in the order stated in the ingredients list and then cover it with the lid.

Pulse for 1 minute until smooth, and then serve.

Nutrition: Calories: 208 Cal; Fat: 0.2 g; Protein: 12.4 g; Carbs: 26.2 g; Fiber: 1.4 g

47   Chocolate Clusters

Preparation Time: 15 minutes

Cooking Time: 0 minutes

Servings: 24

Ingredients:

- 1 cup chopped dark chocolate, vegan
- 1 cup cashews, roasted, salt
- 1 teaspoon sea salt flakes

Directions:

Take a large baking sheet, line it with wax paper, and then set aside until required.

Take a medium bowl, place chocolate in it, and then microwave for 1 minute.

Stir the chocolate and then continue microwaving it at 1-minute intervals until chocolate melts completely, stirring at every interval.

When melted, stir the chocolate to bring it to 90 degrees F and then stir in cashews.

Scoop the walnut-chocolate mixture on the prepared baking sheet, ½ tablespoons per cluster, and then sprinkle with salt.

Let the clusters stand at room temperature until harden and then serve.

Nutrition: Calories: 79.4 Cal; Fat: 6.6 g; Protein: 1 g; Carbs: 5.8 g; Fiber: 1.1 g

48   Banana Coconut Cookies

Preparation Time: 40 minutes

Cooking Time: 0 minutes

Servings: 8

Ingredients:

- 1 ½ cup shredded coconut, unsweetened
- 1 cup mashed banana

Directions:

Switch on the oven, then set it to 350 degrees F and let it preheat.

Take a medium bowl, place the mashed banana in it and then stir in coconut until well combined.

Take a large baking sheet, line it with a parchment sheet, and then scoop the prepared mixture on it, 2 tablespoons of mixture per cookie.

Place the baking sheet into the refrigerator and then let it cool for 30 minutes or more until harden.

Serve straight away.

Nutrition: Calories: 51 Cal; Fat: 3 g; Protein: 0.2 g; Carbs: 4 g; Fiber: 1 g

49   Chocolate Pots

Preparation Time: 4 hours and 10 minutes

Cooking Time: 3 minutes

Yields: 4

Ingredients:

- 6 ounces chocolate, unsweetened
- 1 cup Medjool dates, pitted
- 1 ¾ cups almond milk, unsweetened

Directions:

Cut the chocolate into small pieces, place them in a heatproof bowl and then microwave for 2 to 3 minutes until melt completely, stirring every minute.

lace dates in a blender, pour in the milk, and then pulse until smooth.

Add chocolate into the blender and then pulse until combined.

Divide the mixture into the small mason jars and then let them rest for 4 hours until set.

Serve straight away.

Nutrition: Calories: 321 Cal; Fat: 19 g; Protein: 6 g; Carbs: 34 g; Fiber: 4 g

50   Maple and Tahini Fudge

Preparation Time: 1 hour and 100 minutes

Cooking Time: 3 minutes

Servings: 15

Ingredients:

- 1 cup dark chocolate chips, vegan
- ¼ cup maple syrup
- ½ cup tahini

Directions:

Take a heatproof bowl, place chocolate chips in it and then microwave for 2 to 3 minutes until melt completely, stirring every minute.

When melted, remove the chocolate bowl from the oven and then whisk in maple syrup and tahini until smooth.

Take a 4-by-8 inches baking dish, line it with wax paper, spoon the chocolate mixture in it and then press it into the baking dish.

Cover with another sheet with wax paper, press it down until smooth, and then let the fudge rest for 1 hour in the freezer until set.

Then cut the fudge into 15 squares and serve.

Nutrition: Calories: 110.7 Cal; Fat: 5.3 g; Protein: 2.2 g; Carbs: 15.1 g; Fiber: 1.6 g

Conclusion

In a nutshell, this cookbook offers you a world full of options to diversify your plant-based menu. People on this diet are usually seen struggling to choose between healthy food and flavor but, soon, they run out of the options. The selection of 50 recipes in this book is enough to adorn your dinner table with flavorsome, plant-based meals every day. Give each recipe a good read and try them out in the kitchen. You will experience tempting aromas and binding flavors every day.

The book is conceptualized with the idea of offering you a comprehensive view of a plant-based diet and how it can benefit the body. You may find the shift sudden, especially if you are a die-hard fan of non-vegetarian items. But you need not give up anything that you love. Eat everything in moderation.

The next step is to start experimenting with the different recipes in this book and see which ones are your favorites. Everyone has their favorite food, and you will surely find several of yours in this book. Start with breakfast and work your way through. You will be pleasantly surprised at how tasty a vegan meal really can be.

You will love reading this book, as it helps you to understand how revolutionary a plant-based diet can be. It will help you to make informed decisions as you move toward greater change for the greater good. What are you waiting for? Have you begun your journey on the path of the plant-based diet yet? If you haven't, do it now!

Now you have everything you need to get started making budget-friendly, healthy plant-based recipes. Just follow your basic shopping list and follow your meal plan to get started! It's easy to switch over to a plant-based diet if you have your meals planned out and temptation locked away. Don't forget to clean out your kitchen before starting, and you're sure to meet all your diet and health goals.

You need to plan if you are thinking about dieting. First, you can start slowly by just eating one meal a day, which is vegetarian and gradually increasing your number of vegetarian meals. Whenever you are struggling, ask your friend or family member to support you and keep you motivated. One important thing is also to be regularly accountable for not following the diet.

If dieting seems very important to you and you need to do it right, then it is recommended that you visit a professional such as a nutritionist or dietitian to discuss your dieting plan and optimizing it for the better.

No matter how much you want to lose weight, it is not advised that you decrease your calorie intake to an unhealthy level. Losing weight does not mean that you stop eating. It is done by carefully planning meals.

A plant-based diet is very easy once you get into it. At first, you will start to face a lot of difficulties, but if you start slowly, then you can face all the barriers and achieve your goal.

Swap out one unhealthy food item each week that you know is not helping you and put in its place one of the plant-based ingredients that you like. Then have some fun creating the many different recipes in this book. Find out what recipes you like the most so you can make them often and most of all; have some fun exploring all your recipe options.

Wish you good luck with the plant-based diet!

Notes:

Lightning Source UK Ltd.
Milton Keynes UK
UKHW020654210521
384116UK00005B/150